Life in the
THIRTEEN COLONIES

Delaware

Richard Worth

children's press®
An imprint of
SCHOLASTIC

Library of Congress Cataloging-in-Publication Data

Worth, Richard.
    Delaware / by Richard Worth.
        p. cm. — (Life in the thirteen colonies)
    Includes bibliographical references and index.
    ISBN 0-516-24569-4
    1. Delaware—History—Colonial period, ca. 1600-1775—Juvenile literature. 2. Delaware—History—1775-
1865—Juvenile literature. I. Title. II. Series.
    F167.W67 2004
    975.1'02—dc22

                              2004007458

A Creative Media Applications Production
Design: Fabia Wargin Design
Production: Alan Barnett, Inc.
Editor: Matt Levine
Copy Editor: Laurie Lieb
Proofreader: Tania Bissell
Content Research: Lauren Thogersen
Photo Researcher: Annette Cyr
Content Consultant: David Silverman, Ph.D.

Photo Credits © 2004

Cover: Top left © North Wind Archives; Top right © Francis G. Mayer/CORBIS; Bottom left © Getty Images/Hulton Archive;
Bottom right © North Wind Archives; Background © North Wind Archives; Title page © North Wind Archives; p. 2 © North
Wind Archives; p. 5 © North Wind Archives; p. 8 © North Wind Archives; p. 11 © Getty Images/Hulton Archive; p. 13 ©
North Wind Archives; p. 18 © North Wind Archives; p. 21 © North Wind Archives; p. 22 © Lee Snider; Lee Snider/CORBIS;
p. 24 © North Wind Archives; p. 26 © North Wind Archives; p. 32 © North Wind Archives; p. 34 © North Wind Archives;
p. 39 © North Wind Archives; p. 41 © Museum of the City of New York/CORBIS; p. 42 © North Wind Archives; p. 44 ©
North Wind Archives; p. 49 © North Wind Archives; p. 52 © North Wind Archives; p. 55 © Getty Images/Hulton Archive; p.
56 © North Wind Archives; p. 58: Bottom left © North Wind Archives; Center © Colonial Williamsburg Foundation; Top right
© Jacqui Hurst/CORBIS; Bottom right © Royalty-Free/CORBIS; p. 59: Top left © Historical Picture Archive/CORBIS; Top
right © Bettmann/CORBIS; Bottom left © Bettmann/CORBIS; Bottom right © Colonial Williamsburg Foundation; p. 60 ©
Getty Images/Hulton Archive; p. 63 © Bettmann/CORBIS; p. 66 © Getty Images/Hulton Archive; p. 71 © North Wind
Archives; p. 72 © North Wind Archives; p. 75 © Getty Images/Hulton Archive; p. 78 © North Wind Archives; p. 81 © North
Wind Archives; p. 82 © North Wind Archives; p. 85 © North Wind Archives; p. 88 © Bettmann/CORBIS; p. 91 © Picture
History LLC; p. 93 © North Wind Archives; p. 95 © North Wind Archives; p. 98 © North Wind Archives; p. 100 © North
Wind Archives; p. 103 © North Wind Archives; p. 104 © North Wind Archives; p. 107 © North Wind Archives; p. 108 ©
North Wind Archives; p. 114 © North Wind Archives; p. 118: Top left © North Wind Archives; Bottom left © North Wind
Archives; Bottom right © North Wind Archives; p. 119: Top right © North Wind Archives; Bottom left © Getty
Images/Hulton Archive; Bottom right © North Wind Archives; Background © North Wind Archives

CONTENTS

THE
ORIGINAL
THIRTEEN COLONIES,
1775

NEW FRANCE

MAINE
(part of Mass.)

St. Lawrence River

Lake Champlain

Lake Ontario

Lake Erie

NEW HAMPSHIRE

Falmouth

Portsmouth
Newburyport

Mohawk R.

Albany

Salem
Boston

MASSACHUSETTS

Cape Cod

NEW YORK

Hudson R.

Connecticut River

Hartford

New Haven

Newport

RHODE ISLAND

CONNECTICUT

Long Island

Delaware R.

New York

Susquehanna R.

Perth Amboy

PENNSYLVANIA

Philadelphia

Burlington

Pittsburgh

York

New Castle

NEW JERSEY

Appalachian Mountains

Ohio River

Baltimore

Potomac R.

MARYLAND

DELAWARE

Alexandria

Atlantic Ocean

James River

Richmond

Chesapeake Bay

Williamsburg

VIRGINIA

Norfolk

Roanoke River

Edenton

Hillsboro

Halifax

Cape Hatteras

Salem

NORTH CAROLINA

Bath

New Bern

Pamlico Sound

Salisbury

Charlotte

Cross Creek

Cape Fear R.

Camden

Wilmington

SOUTH CAROLINA

Georgetown

Augusta

Savannah River

GEORGIA

Charles Town

Savannah

NORTH

EAST

WEST

SOUTH

SPANISH TERRITORY

Legend

Colonial boundaries
(The western boundaries of many
colonies were undefined in 1775.)

0   125   250
Scale in Miles

A Nation Grows
From Thirteen Colonies

Delaware lies in the mid-Atlantic region of the United States. Its eastern border is formed by Delaware Bay and the Atlantic Ocean. It is surrounded on the west and south by Maryland and borders Pennsylvania and New Jersey in the north.

Early settlers came from Sweden, Ireland, Finland, and England. For hundreds of years before these Europeans arrived, Delaware was home to the Lenni-Lenape Indians. Their culture was eventually pushed aside by the newcomers.

Delaware Bay provided both rich farmland and a safe harbor for the new colonists. When the American colonies decided to break away from England, Delaware sent many of its citizens to fight for the new nation. It was the first of the original thirteen colonies to sign the **Constitution**.

The map shows the thirteen English colonies in 1775. The colored sections show the areas that were settled at that time.

CHAPTER ONE

Early European Explorers

Early Exploration

The Native Americans of the area now called Delaware may have seen a European sailing ship passing by their shores as early as 1524. That year, Italian explorer Giovanni da Verrazano sailed his ship, *La Dauphine*, north along the North American coast, from present-day South Carolina to New York. Along the way, he passed the area now known as Delaware Bay.

Over the next few decades, English and Dutch explorers also made voyages to the New World. (Europeans considered Europe the Old World. They called North and South America the New World.) One of the major goals of these trips was finding a shorter route from Europe to Asia. For centuries, spices, silks, and precious gems had been brought

European explorers traveled along the Delaware coast in sailing ships such as this during the 1500s.

from China and India to Europe by land and water routes that were long and dangerous. Many Europeans believed that a faster water route through the North American continent existed. If this route could be found, greater riches would follow.

Henry Hudson Sails for North America

In 1553, a group of English merchants formed the Muscovy Company to search for this route, called the Northwest Passage. They hired a young sea captain named Henry Hudson to lead an **expedition** to the New World. In 1607, Hudson left England aboard the ship *Hopewell*, in search of the Northwest Passage.

The *Hopewell* sailed north toward Greenland, where it ran into dense fog, snow, freezing rain, and large icebergs. Fearing his ship would be crushed by the monstrous chunks of ice, Hudson turned the *Hopewell* around and headed back to England.

Hudson attempted one more expedition for the Muscovy Company, but again failed to find the shortcut. The company refused to finance another expedition, and so on Hudson's third voyage, in 1609, he sailed under the Dutch flag. The Dutch were developing a great trading **empire,** and by 1600 had as many as 10,000 ships trading in Europe.

The English sailor Henry Hudson explored the Atlantic coast of America and traded with the native people there.

With a Dutch and English crew, Hudson set sail in his ship, the *Half Moon*, in early April. In July, he reached the coast of Newfoundland. The following month, he sailed south past present-day Cape Cod, Massachusetts, and reached what is now called Delaware Bay.

Hudson continued as far south as Virginia and then reversed course and returned to Delaware Bay. He then sailed north into what is now New York Harbor and up the river that would one day be named after him. Hudson never found the shortcut, but he claimed the land around New York Harbor for his Dutch employers.

When he returned home, Hudson told the Dutch about his discoveries and about the people, animals, and fertile land in America. The Europeans were especially interested in the beavers and other fur-bearing animals. The **pelts** from these animals were very valuable. They were used to make hats and other clothing. Hudson's discoveries would spur the Dutch and other countries to establish colonies in the New World.

The Lenni-Lenape

Before the arrival of the Europeans, the area now known as Delaware was inhabited by Native Americans. The main tribe in this area, with a population of about 20,000, was the Lenni-Lenape. The word *Lenni-Lenape* means "original people." Their lives revolved around farming and the cycles of the seasons. They grew corn, squash, beans, and sweet potatoes and hunted and fished around the Delaware River.

Farming and Cooking

Lenni-Lenape women were in charge of planting seeds in the spring, tending the fields throughout the summer, and harvesting the crops each fall. These tasks took so much

The main food crop for the Lenni-Lenape was corn. Everyone in the tribe helped plant and harvest the crop. But women were responsible for tending the corn fields and making sure there was a good harvest.

time that women often carried their newborn babies while working. The babies were strapped into cradle-boards, pieces of wood with leather straps to hold the babies tightly. The women wore the cradle-boards on their backs while working in the fields.

Girls helped their mothers and learned to tend the fields. They also were taught to cook many dishes, including corn bread and succotash, a mixture of corn and beans. Lenni-Lenape women did much of their cooking inside houses called wigwams, which were framed with wooden poles and covered with bark. A hole at the top of each structure allowed smoke from cooking fires to escape. Some of the wigwams were circular with round roofs, while others were rectangular with arched roofs.

Hunting and Fishing

While girls learned from their mothers, boys spent most of their time with their fathers. Lenni-Lenape men were responsible for hunting and fishing, and they taught these skills to their sons. Villages of about fifty wigwams were located along rivers and bays to ensure that the Indians had a plentiful supply of fish close at hand.

Indian men also taught their sons how to build dugout canoes that could be paddled along the rivers while fishing. These 20-foot (6-meter) canoes were made by burning and then hollowing out cedar logs or other tree trunks. The men used nets or wooden traps called weirs to catch their fish. Indian boys also learned to spear fish with harpoons made from deer antlers. Once a fish was caught, it was cleaned, wrapped in clay, and cooked in the warm ashes from a fire. Then the clay was broken open and the family enjoyed a delicious fish dinner.

Men also hunted game birds like geese, ducks, and wild turkeys using bows and arrows. Making bows and arrows from tree branches and sharp stones was one of the many lessons that Indian boys received from their fathers. They

Lenni-Lenape Games

Recreation was a big part of Lenni-Lanape life. The Indians enjoyed a variety of games, including a cross between football and soccer, in which men played against women. The men could only kick the ball, which was made out of animal skin, but the women could also throw the ball and run with it. Each team tried to drive the ball through a set of goalposts.

The Lenni-Lenape also enjoyed a game called Mamandin, played with dice made from animal bones. Another game, called Selahtikan, was a forerunner of the modern game of pick-up sticks. Using pieces of reeds, the Indians tried to pick up one of the reed sticks without moving any of the others.

also learned how to walk quietly through the woods, so their prey would not hear them. A common trick Indian hunters used was to set fire to an area of woodland in order to drive out any animals that might be hiding there, making them easy targets. Never wasteful with the animals they killed, the natives used deer for more than food. Antlers and bones were made into tools, fishhooks, and arrowheads. Deerskins were made into clothing like leggings and moccasins. Besides their characteristic clothing, Lenni-Lenape men wore their hair in a special style. They pulled most of the hair from their heads, but left a tuft of hair in the middle. This tuft, called a scalp lock, was greased so that it stood upright.

Other Lenape Customs

Some Lenni-Lenape men served as sachems, or chiefs, of the tribe. Each sachem was in charge of several villages. Other tribes called the Lenni-Lenape "grandfathers" out of respect for their wisdom. The Lenni-Lenape sachems were relied upon to help find peaceful solutions to conflicts among the tribes.

When a tribe member was killed by an enemy, the Lenni-Lenape would declare war to avenge the killing. But the Lenni-Lenape were generally a peaceful people. They preferred social gatherings and celebrations to warfare.

Lenni-Lenape Myths

The Lenni-Lenape believed in an all-powerful creator god, called Kishelemukong. They told many stories about the creator, including one called "When Squirrels Were Huge." According to the story, squirrels were once enormous animals that would attack any other creatures in the forest and eat them. No one was safe, including the creator god's own child, who was killed by a huge squirrel. When Kishelemukong found out what the squirrel had done, he roared in a powerful voice that blew through the branches of the trees and made the earth move. "Now, from this time on," the god shouted, "it is you who will be little and your children and your great-grandchildren will be eaten." This is how the squirrel lost its powerful position on earth and was replaced by humans.

Some Lenni-Lenape homes had pictures of spirits carved on their doorways. This fire-breathing creature may have represented the Great Horned Serpent.

They danced to music made by water drums, wooden drums partly filled with water and covered with deerskin.

These customs would soon begin to change. Over the next two centuries, life as the Lenni-Lenape had always known it would be transformed by the arrival of great numbers of Europeans.

11

Further European Exploration

Henry Hudson's 1609 voyage to the New World was soon followed by other expeditions, mostly from England. That same year, British captain Samuel Argall sailed to the Jamestown colony in Virginia. With the help of Virginia's governor, Baron De La Warr, Argall built forts at Jamestown to defend the colony against attacks by Indians and pirates. He then sailed to the British colony of Bermuda to get supplies.

Along the way, Argall was blown off course, and in 1610, he reached the bay that Hudson had entered a year earlier. Argall named it Delaware Bay, after the Virginia governor ("De La Warr" became "Delaware"). He also explored the river that ran into the bay. He called it the Delaware River. Captain Argall gave the same name to the Indians he encountered living along the bay. In truth, these were members of the Lenni-Lenape tribe, but Argall, not knowing their tribal name, called them the Delaware.

Following Argall's voyage, the Delaware area was visited by other Dutch explorers, including Cornelis Hendricksen in 1616 and Cornelis Jacobsen May in 1620. The Dutch would eventually establish a colony there. A year after May's visit, the Dutch set up the Dutch West India Company to control all of the European trade with Dutch colonies in the New World.

Samuel Argall explored Delaware Bay and named it for the governor of Virginia, Baron De La Warr.

Dutch Settlement

The company was given the land in North America that had been claimed by Henry Hudson for the Dutch government. They named the territory New Netherland. (New Netherland was named for the Netherlands, another name for the country also known as Holland, where the Dutch people lived.)

Early in the 1620s, Dutch settlers began to establish farms along the Hudson River. By 1626, the governor of

How the Delaware Got Their Name

The Lenni-Lenape have their own story about the way in which they came to be named the Delaware. They believe that the Europeans asked the Indians the name of their tribe. The answer was "Lenape." But the Europeans, unable to pronounce that name, kept calling the Indians "Lenuhpee" or "Renahpay."

Eventually, the white men got the name right, and the Lenape shouted, "Nal ne ndeluwen! Nal ne ndeluwen!" which in their language means, "That's what I said!" The Europeans, however, mistakenly heard the Indians say "deluwen" and took that to be their name. The Europeans pronounced it "Delaware." The Lenape accepted this name and used it when they dealt with the white settlers. But among themselves, the Indians continued to use their traditional name, Lenape.

New Netherland had sent settlers south to the Delaware River to establish a trading post called Fort Nassau. From there, they hoped to trade with the Delaware Indians for beaver fur to meet the great demand for fur in Europe. Wealthy Europeans craved warm fur hats and coats to withstand the cold winters. This first settlement along the Delaware would soon be followed by others.

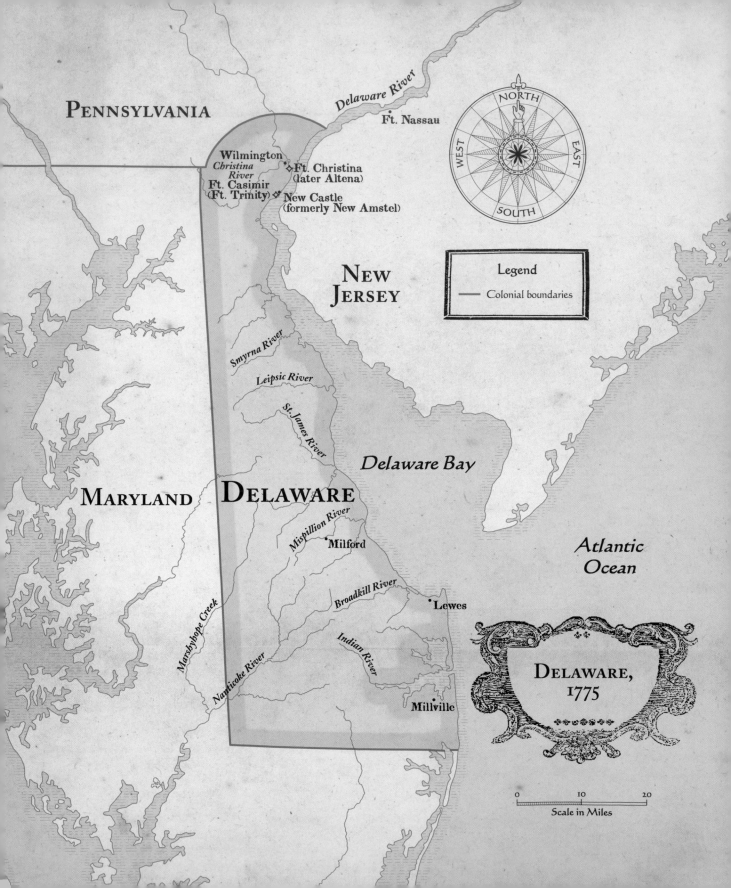

PENNSYLVANIA

Delaware River

Ft. Nassau

Wilmington
Christina River
Ft. Casimir
(Ft. Trinity)

◇ Ft. Christina
(later Altena)

New Castle
(formerly New Amstel)

NORTH
WEST EAST
SOUTH

Legend
— Colonial boundaries

NEW
JERSEY

Smyrna River

Leipsic River

St. James River

MARYLAND

DELAWARE

Delaware Bay

Mispillion River
• Milford

Broadkill River

Marshyhope Creek

Indian River

• Lewes

Nanticoke River

*Atlantic
Ocean*

DELAWARE,
1775

• Millville

0   10   20
Scale in Miles

CHAPTER TWO
Contest for Control

The Indians and the Dutch

As more Dutch settled near Delaware Bay during the 1630s, they soon came into conflict with the Lenni-Lenape. In 1631, a sailing ship named the *Whale* appeared in Delaware Bay. On board were twenty-eight men from the Netherlands who hoped to set up a new colony. They carried bricks to construct buildings, farm animals to provide the settlers with food, and equipment to catch whales that lived in the bay.

The settlers called their new colony Zwaanendael, which means the Valley of the Swans, named for the many swans living along the coast. Cutting down huge trees, the Dutch settlers cleared a section of the forest. They built houses to live in and a cookhouse to boil the whale blubber and extract the oil, which was used in lamps. They also built a wooden wall, called a palisade, to surround and protect the buildings from attacks by Indians.

This map shows how Delaware looked in 1775.

The Dutch quickly set up a brisk trade with the Lenni-Lenape, exchanging hatchets, mirrors, combs, iron pots, and smoking pipes for fish and deer meat. The Indians also liked a special kind of woolen cloth that the Dutch brought. Called *duffel*, it began to replace deerskins in the making of Indian clothing. Once the colony had been set up, the *Whale* returned to Holland to bring back more supplies.

When David Pietersen De Vries, one of the colony's leaders, arrived the following year, he was horrified by what he found. The entire settlement had been wiped out. Everything had been burned, and the

When De Vries returned to Delaware, he found skeletons of the settlers in the burned settlement.

charred skulls of settlers lay scattered on the ground. De Vries eventually learned what had happened to the colony from the Lenni-Lenape.

The massacre had occurred when a Lenape sachem took a tin medallion from the settlement. He thought the metal could be used to make a fine pipe for smoking tobacco. When the colonists complained to the Indians about this thief, the Indians executed the sachem because they did not want the settlers to stop trading with them. The execution enraged friends of the sachem, so they burned down the Dutch settlement. Discouraged by the destruction of his colony, De Vries and his companions returned to Holland.

The Dutch and the Swedish

The next attempt to set up a colony in what is now Delaware was financed by a group of investors from Holland and Sweden. Since the sixteenth century, the Dutch and the Swedes had maintained close trading ties. In fact, Dutch ships carried the majority of trade goods to and from Sweden. Several Dutch colonial leaders had become frustrated with unsuccessful efforts to establish a colony on Delaware Bay. One of these leaders, Peter Minuit, decided to try on his own.

Minuit had served as governor of the Dutch colony of New Netherland. But he had been fired by the Dutch West India Company and sent back to Holland. He now wanted to establish a colony to compete with the Dutch West India Company. Minuit also believed that a colony south of New Amsterdam (New Netherland's chief city, which would one day become New York City) would have a good climate for growing tobacco, a valuable crop that could be sold in Europe.

In 1632, the New Sweden Company was established by Minuit and a group of Swedish investors. One of its goals was to set up a new colony in Delaware. Six years later, Minuit led an expedition of two ships, the *Kalmar Nyckel* and the *Grippen*, across the stormy Atlantic Ocean to Delaware Bay.

New Sweden

Minuit landed his ships south of the area where the Dutch had established Fort Nassau on the Delaware River. There, he bartered with the Lenni-Lenape, trading European goods in exchange for a large tract of land. The Swedish settlers, who were mainly soldiers, built a fort on the land that Minuit named Fort Christina, after the queen of Sweden. During their first year at Fort Christina, the Swedes traded with the Lenni-Lenape and other Indian tribes for animal pelts. As a result, 2,200 beaver, otter, and bear pelts were packed onto ships and sent back to Europe. On one of these return trips, Minuit's ship went down in a violent hurricane, and he drowned.

The New Sweden Company selected a new leader, Peter Ridder, a Swedish naval officer. In 1640, Ridder arrived in New Sweden, bringing additional colonists. They began to lay out farms around Fort Christina where the settlers would grow wheat and tobacco.

Governor Johan Printz

Ridder was replaced in 1643 by another military officer, Johan Printz, who would become New Sweden's most successful governor. The Indians called the new governor "big tub" or "big belly," because Printz was a huge man, weighing close to 400 pounds (180 kilograms). Printz built additional forts throughout the colony to defend New Sweden from the Dutch, who did not want the colony so close to New Netherland. Although the Dutch and the Swedish were trading partners, they were still competing for control of colonies in the New World.

At the same time that he was defending his colony against the Dutch, Printz also had to deal with the English. A group of English colonists from Connecticut, calling themselves the Delaware Company of New Haven, wanted a part of New Sweden's valuable fur trade.

Governor Printz acted quickly to build a fort to defend New Sweden from the Dutch and the English.

They also hoped to establish tobacco farms in Delaware. George Lamberton of the Delaware Company led an expedition to the Delaware River to found three settlements. Acting swiftly, Printz arrested Lamberton, charging him with illegal fur trading and encouraging the Indians to revolt against the Swedes. Lamberton was tried, found guilty, fined, and forced to leave New Sweden in 1643. Meanwhile, the fur trade and

A log cabin built in the early 1700s by Swedish settlers still stands at Fort Christina, the first permanent European settlement in Delaware.

tobacco business flourished. In 1643, Printz sent more than 2,000 fur pelts and 20,000 pounds (4,000 kilograms) of tobacco to Europe for sale.

Printz built himself a governor's house on Tinicum Island in the Delaware River. The house had rooms for the governor's family as well as offices where the business of the colony was conducted. He moved the capital of the colony from Fort Christina to this new house, which he called New Gothenburg.

By 1647, only 183 people were living in New Sweden. Printz wanted more settlers there to strengthen the colony. Fearing a conflict with the Indians, he also asked the directors of the New Sweden Company for more soldiers. As he put it, "Nothing would be better than that a couple of hundred soldiers should be sent here and kept here until we broke the necks of all of them [Indians] in the river.... They are a lot of poor rascals." But Printz never got his additional soldiers, and eventually this cost him control of the colony.

Along with the Swedish settlers was a group of people from the country of Finland, which is near Sweden. The Finns were a helpful addition to the young colony because they knew how to build new settlements quickly. In their cold, densely wooded homeland, the Finns learned how to cut down trees. Then they trimmed the trees, cut notches in each end, and fit them together. This quick but secure method of house construction prevented drafts.

Settlers from Finland built the first log cabins in New Sweden using the many trees they found in the Delaware River valley.

The Growth of New Sweden

When they came to New Sweden, the Finnish settlers introduced this same type of wooden home to the colony. It soon became known as a log cabin. A small door opening carved in the front was covered with a wooden slab on hinges. Wood was also placed across the windows to keep out cold drafts during the winter.

The log cabin's roof was made out of flat clapboards, held down by long poles called weight poles, which were laid across the roof. Inside the house, a clay fireplace with a wooden chimney was used for cooking and heating the home. Most colonists slept on straw or leaves on the floor, except those few who could afford beds.

In addition to log cabins, the Swedes and Finns also constructed saunas, called *bastus*, which were built near rivers. Inside one of these wooden buildings, the colonists constructed a huge fireplace. When it got very hot with a roaring fire, they poured water over the fireplace stones to create steam. Then they lay on wooden shelves, enjoying their steam bath as it gently moistened their skin.

Finnish settlers cut the dense forest to clear farmland. They built homes and fences with the wood from the trees.

The New Sweden colonists also built a mill for cutting wood. They used wood to build their homes, to make furniture and wooden ploughs for farming, and even to create wooden eating utensils. They also built a brewery, where they made beer from wheat grown in their fields.

Trouble on the Horizon

As New Sweden grew, Governor Printz had to deal with the Dutch in New Netherland who wanted to take control of his colony. In 1651, New Netherland governor Peter Stuyvesant decided to take action. With a fleet of eleven ships and an army of 120 soldiers, he sailed to Delaware Bay. There, Stuyvesant met with the Lenni-Lenape Indians and demanded that they sell the Dutch more land on the Delaware River.

The Indians had already sold this land to the Swedes. They did not want to offend Stuyvesant, so they gave him the land as a gift rather than selling it to him. To the Lenape, this made perfect sense. When they sold land, they considered that they were just selling the right to use the land. They expected to be able to continue to use it themselves and to allow others to do the same. When the European settlers bought land, however, they thought that no one else could use it. This was an important difference between the Indians and the settlers.

Stuyvesant thought he now owned the land given to him by the Lenape. He constructed a new Dutch **outpost** called Fort Casimir south of the Swedish Fort Christina. Fort Casimir was protected by wooden palisades and cannons that could fire on any ship that sailed into Delaware Bay on its way to the Delaware River. The colony of New Sweden now had an enemy right on its doorstep, and there was nothing that Printz could do about it. He simply did not have enough soldiers.

Striking at the Dutch

Governor Printz realized that the situation in New Sweden was growing dangerous. He had too few men to stop the Dutch from conquering the colony. He wrote home for more colonists, supplies, and soldiers to strengthen the colony, but he received little help.

The colonists began complaining that Printz was driving them to work too hard with too little food. In 1653, a revolt began, led by a settler named Anders Jonsson. Printz arrested Jonsson, held a trial, and executed him. While this put an end to the revolt, Printz came to realize that he did not have the resources to govern the colony any longer. Late in 1653, he and his family sailed home to Sweden. He was replaced as governor by Johan Rising, who arrived in the New World in 1654 aboard his ship, the *Orn*. Rising immediately decided to strike a blow against the Dutch in an attempt to save New Sweden.

There were very few soldiers at the Dutch outpost at Fort Casimir. Rising sailed up to Fort Casimir in his heavily armed ship. The Dutch, realizing that they could not put up a fight, surrendered. Rising renamed the fort Trinity.

Making Soap

Colonists had to make most of the things they needed in their daily lives. One of these was soap. To make soap, the only necessary ingredients were wood ashes and animal fat.

First the colonists poured water over the ashes from a wood fire. The brown liquid that oozed out of the ashes is called potash lye. Next animal fat was boiled with water and left to cool overnight. The fat that floated to the top of this slimy mixture was scooped off. Since the process was very smelly, this step was always done outside the home.

Finally, the fat and potash were combined with water in a large kettle and boiled. When the foamy mixture seemed just right, a brave colonist dipped his or her finger into the ooze and tasted it. If it stung the tongue just a little bit, the soap was done.

The soap was allowed to cool before it was poured into barrels. Colonial soap was a brown, jelly-like substance that was scooped from a container when needed. The soap worked well to keep things clean.

However, this victory against the Dutch did not solve the serious problems in New Sweden.

In his first report on the state of the colony, Rising wrote that more skilled **artisans** were needed. He asked for more timber cutters, a soap maker, pottery makers, cabinetmakers, and shoemakers. Rising also told the directors of the New Sweden Company that the colony would make more money if it started a brewery, an inn for travelers, and a mill to make gunpowder.

The governor also said that the forts needed more cannons so the colonists could defend themselves in case they were attacked. "We have therefore borrowed four [cannons] from the ship," he wrote, "and placed them in an entrenchment before the fort, the better to sweep the river straight across."

The Conquest of New Sweden

A major Dutch attack finally came in 1655. Stuyvesant and 400 soldiers sailed up to Fort Trinity and surrounded it. The Swedes had seventy-five soldiers to defend the fort. They were no match for the Dutch army.

Stuyvesant put his troops between the two forts so that no other Swedish soldiers could help. Realizing that he was outgunned, Fort Trinity's commander decided not to fight. He surrendered the fort to the Dutch on September 1, 1655. After this victory, Stuyvesant and the Dutch marched northward and attacked Fort Christina. The Dutch surrounded the fort, burned the Swedish settlements, and killed the farm animals.

At first, Governor Rising had planned to defend Fort Christina, but his soldiers had very little ammunition. Rising later wrote that after two weeks,

We then assembled a general council of
the whole garrison, and it was found to be their
unanimous opinion, that inasmuch as we had
not sufficient strength for our defense...and were
in want both of powder and other munitions,
and had no hope of relief, therefore they were
all of opinion, that we should make the best
terms we could obtain with the Dutch.

Meanwhile, Stuyvesant had received an urgent message from New Netherland about an Indian uprising that was threatening that colony. Stuyvesant realized that he might be forced to call off his siege of Fort Christina. He offered to let Rising continue to govern the colony if he returned Fort Trinity to the Dutch without any more fighting.

Rising refused, saying that he was not authorized to give up Fort Trinity and that the Swedes could no longer survive in the colony because their homes and livestock had been destroyed. Stuyvesant continued to surround the fort. On September 15, 1655, Rising surrendered, and the Dutch took control of the entire New Sweden colony. The Swedes had lost their colony and their foothold in the New World.

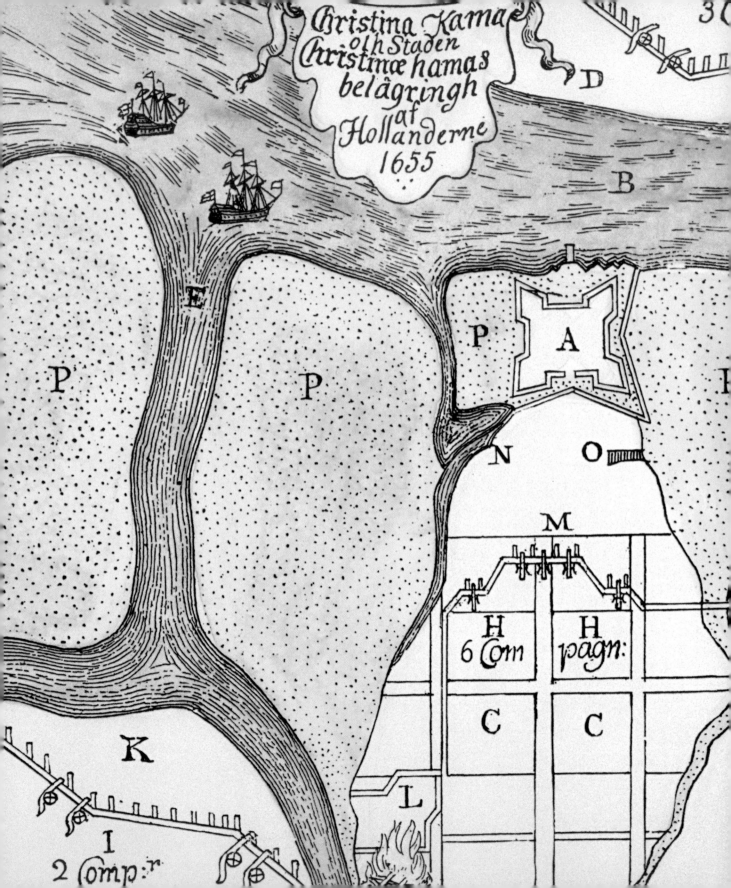

Christina Kama
och Staden
Christinæ hamas
belägringh
af
Hollanderne
1655

3C

D

B

E

P

P

P

A

N O

M

H H
6 Com pagn:

C C

K

L

I
2 Comp:r

CHAPTER THREE

England Against the Netherlands

Delaware under the Dutch

After his victory over the Swedes, Peter Stuyvesant returned home to New Amsterdam. He was very proud of his expansion of the Dutch territory in the New World, which now included New Netherland and New Sweden.

Stuyvesant had spent much of his life working for the Dutch West India Company. In addition to running colonies, the Dutch West India Company was also involved in the slave trade. The company set up outposts on the western coast of Africa and traded with local tribes for slaves.

During the 1650s, the company transported these slaves to the Caribbean and to Dutch colonies in New Netherland and along the Delaware River. Dutch ships regularly sailed

◁ This map shows Fort Christina in 1655. The fort is labeled with the letter A on the map.

out of New Amsterdam and brought back slaves to work on the tobacco plantations that were rapidly springing up along the Delaware River. The Swedish settlers bought slaves from the Dutch slave traders.

Slaves were brought to New Sweden to make up for the small number of settlers who were moving there from Europe. But by the late 1650s, the Dutch government had encouraged more **immigrants** from Sweden and Finland to go to New Sweden because the Dutch were desperate for new colonists.

During the 1650s, ships brought new settlers to New Sweden. They established the town of New Amstel not far from Fort Casimir.

Many of these new arrivals settled around a new city called New Amstel, which was near Fort Casimir. New Amstel became the capital of New Sweden. Here, the Dutch erected a church, a tavern, and several rows of houses built of planks and logs. The roofs were made out of tiles, boards, and straw.

In Holland, the Dutch had created dikes, barriers of built-up earth, to keep water from flooding their towns. In New Amstel, dikes were built to protect the houses and fields from being flooded by the waters of Delaware Bay. Roads were built along the tops of the dikes so settlers could travel easily from one farm to another.

The City Colony

The city of Amsterdam in Holland also encouraged people to move to New Amstel. Amsterdam, a thriving center of trade and finance, was one of the wealthiest cities in Europe. In 1656, the city made a deal with the Dutch West India Company to take over the southern part of New Sweden, including New Amstel.

This new section, run by the leaders of the city of Amsterdam, was called the City Colony. The northern part of New Sweden, called the Company Colony, remained under the control of the Dutch West India Company. This part of the colony had its capital at old Fort Christina, which the Dutch now called Altena.

Amsterdam merchants encouraged residents of Holland to go to live in New Amstel by offering them free land in the colony. They also loaned them money for the trip to North America. A new governor, Jacob Alrichs, made New Amstel larger by building a town hall and new wooden wharves along the Delaware River. In 1658, the first schoolmaster, Evert Pietersen, came to New Amstel to teach Dutch children to read and write.

Fence and Tobacco Inspectors

The governors of New Amstel encouraged a limited form of **democratic** government in the colony. The settlers gathered together in a town meeting to select local officials, including two fence inspectors and four tobacco inspectors.

Worm Fence

The split rail or worm fence was the most popular fence built by early settlers. It was called a worm fence because it appeared to zigzag across the countryside like a worm.

Many trees were required to create posts and rails for a worm fence.

It took 1 acre (0.4 hectares) of trees to make enough rails and posts for about 10 acres (4 hectares) of land. Each rail was cut about four ax handles long, or about 11 feet (3 meters). A common way to measure a field was to count the rails that surrounded it.

The fence inspectors played an important role in colonial New Amstel. They made sure that each farm had a stable fence around it. The fence prevented pigs, goats, and other farm animals from straying off a farmer's land and wandering into a neighbor's field, where they might dig up corn or other crops. The tobacco inspectors were needed to determine the size of each planter's tobacco crop so a fair tax could be paid on it.

In addition, the governor used the town meeting to win support for making improvements at Fort Casimir. The residents at the town meeting also decided on a price to pay the Indians for the furs that they trapped and sold to the colonists.

The Growth of New Amstel

New Amstel continued to grow during the 1650s, becoming the most important city in what would become present-day Delaware. By 1658, about 600 settlers lived there, many more than when the colony had been under Swedish control.

The colony still faced serious problems. Bad weather reduced the size of the corn harvest, and some of the colonists died from an outbreak of fever. As a result, some left New Amstel, moving north to New Amsterdam or south to the English colony of Maryland. In 1659, Governor Alrichs died and was replaced by Alexander D'Hinoyossa.

The new governor tried to establish trade with the English colonists in Maryland. This plan worked at first but soon fell to ruin, as did Dutch control of the Delaware colonies.

The English Arrive

During much of the seventeenth century, the Netherlands was the greatest trading nation in Europe. From busy port cities such as Amsterdam, Dutch ships carried goods to and from England, France, Norway, Sweden, and Spain. Dutch ships carried Norwegian timber, French wines, and English cloth, charging less than their competitors in the trading business.

The English were intent on stopping the Dutch traders. Beginning in 1651, England passed a series of laws called Navigation Acts, which prevented goods from being brought into England or its colonies except on English ships. The Navigation Acts were aimed directly at hurting

Pirates and Smugglers

The Navigation Acts were aimed at stopping trade between the colonies and nations other than England. But the colonists knew that the British could not watch every ship, port, and dock. As a result, the colonists turned to pirates and smugglers to get things they wanted. These crafty seamen smuggled goods from the Caribbean or other parts of the world into the colonies. Many colonists and even some British merchants got rich selling smuggled goods.

the Dutch traders. As a result, England and Holland fought a series of wars on the ocean from 1652 to 1674. During this period of war, the English decided to take control of the Dutch colonies in North America.

English and Dutch ships fought fierce battles at sea as a result of the Navigation Acts.

Early in the 1660s, the English king, Charles II, gave his brother James, the Duke of York, a large piece of land in North America. It included New Netherland and the Dutch settlements along the Delaware River. To take control of this land, James had to remove the Dutch. James was also the commander of the English fleets. He sent four ships and 400 men, led by Colonel Richard Nicolls, to North America.

Meanwhile, Governor Stuyvesant wanted to strengthen the defenses of New Amsterdam. He was sure that the English were going to strike his colony. But the Dutch government told him not to worry. It was convinced that the Duke of York's army was sailing to the English colonies north of New Netherland.

The English Take Over

Stuyvesant was taken completely off guard when the English fleet sailed into the harbor at New Amsterdam in September 1664. He had no choice but to surrender the city.

Colonel Nicolls then sent two ships and about 200 men south to capture the Dutch colonies along the Delaware. The troops were under the command of Sir Robert Carr. Carr's strategy was to try to divide the colonists. He convinced the Swedes, many of whom still resented the Dutch, that their farms and businesses would be protected if the English took control. Then he went to New Amstel and tried to persuade Governor D'Hinoyossa to surrender. The Dutch leader refused. Carr's soldiers came ashore at Fort Casimir, surrounded the stronghold, and attacked. The Dutch were greatly outnumbered and were easily defeated.

But victory was not enough for the English. They decided to teach the Dutch a lesson for trying to put up a fight against them. Carr's army took all the goods from the storehouses inside the Dutch fort, as well as the sheep, cows, and slaves owned by the Dutch farmers.

English Rule

Now Nicolls was in charge of all the colonies along the Delaware River. He changed the name New Amsterdam to New York. He changed the name of New Amstel to New Castle. He assured the colonists that the English would not interfere with their settlements.

In 1674, Dutch settlers gave the keys to New Netherland, including settlements in Delaware, to the English.

Some of the colonists were not happy about having the English in charge. In 1669, a settler named Marcus Jacobson gathered supporters to oppose the English government. They spoke in taverns and churches, telling people that Swedish ships were sailing to Delaware to take back the colony. When the English heard about this opposition, they arrested Jacobson. He was taken to New York, tried, and found guilty of treason. Jacobson was branded with an *R* on his cheek to show that he was a rebel. He was then sold as a slave in the Caribbean.

By 1673, the English were again at war with the Dutch. That year, a Dutch fleet under the command of Admiral Cornelis Evertsen sailed into New York Harbor. The harbor was not well defended. Evertsen recaptured the city. Then the fleet sailed south and grabbed control of New Castle. After the war, however, the New York and Delaware settlements were soon returned to England as part of a peace treaty signed in 1674. They once again came under the control of the Duke of York.

For the next eight years, the Delaware colony would continue to be governed from New York. In 1681, however, a new era in the history of Delaware began.

Stubborn Pete

Peter Stuyvesant, the governor of New Netherland who constantly threatened Delaware's settlers, had many nicknames. He was called "Stubborn Pete," "Pegleg Pete," and "Old Silverleg." None of the nicknames were meant as a compliment.

Stuyvesant was sent to New Netherland to clean up the Dutch colony and put things in order. He did that quickly, but he made many enemies in the process.

The General, as he liked to be called, had fought for the Dutch West India Company in the Caribbean. A cannonball had blown off his right leg from the knee down. He replaced it with a wooden peg that had silver nails around it. That is how he got two of his nicknames.

Stuyvesant was known for being stubborn and **intolerant**. He hated blacks, Jews, and almost anyone who was not a member of the Dutch Reformed Church. He once had a Quaker farmer who disagreed with him whipped until his own daughter finally pleaded with him to stop. He

Governor Stuyvesant let citizens know when he was angry with them. Here, he yells at a shoemaker in the public square.

traded in slaves and imposed new taxes on the colonists.

All in all, Stuyvesant was thoroughly disliked. But he was also respected by many people because he got things done and kept the colony in good working order. In the end, the Dutch settlers of New Netherland turned against him and surrendered the colony without a fight to the English. They may have thought that anything was better than being ruled by "Stubborn Pete."

Chapter Four

Penn Takes Over

A Transfer of Power

In 1681, William Penn, the founder of the English colony of Pennsylvania, laid claim to the Delaware colony. This bold move led to important changes. In the fall of 1682, Penn sailed from England to New Castle. When he came ashore, he was greeted by two of the local representatives of the Duke of York.

Penn walked quickly to the entrance of old Fort Casimir, entered, and locked the door behind him. When he came out, he was given a porringer (a cup with a handle) containing soil and water from the Delaware River, as well as a piece of ground with a twig on it. These gifts symbolized that he was now the owner of the territory.

William Penn made peace with the Indian tribes of Pennsylvania and Delaware after he took over the territory granted to him by the king of England.

William Penn

William Penn was a member of a distinguished English family. His father, Admiral Sir William Penn, was a friend of King Charles II and the Duke of York. The elder Penn had commanded English fleets in Europe and the Caribbean during the wars with the Dutch and was later appointed a commissioner of the royal navy.

Sir William wanted his son to follow in his footsteps. He sent the younger Penn to Oxford University in 1660 to receive an education that would train him for government service. But the young man had other ideas. As a child, he

The Society of Friends

The name of the Quaker religion is the Religious Society of Friends. They thought everyone should be equal and act as "friends."

Quakers opposed slavery and were against all forms of violence. When Quaker men were ordered to serve in the army, they often refused.

Quakers also believed that the sexes were equal. Most people in colonial times thought that men were superior to women. In Quaker churches, women could speak as freely as men and were often Quaker leaders.

Quakers believed in a simple, honest way of life. Quaker merchants refused to bargain about the price of their goods. They thought bargaining suggested that they were lying when they put a price on something.

had experienced a profound religious awakening, which led him to question the teachings of the Anglican Church. The Anglican Church was the established church of England, supported by the king and his officials. At Oxford, Penn developed friendships with other students who shared his beliefs. He was eventually kicked out of the university because he spoke out against the Anglican Church.

During the 1660s, Penn joined a religious group called the Society of Friends. They were also known as the Quakers because they were said to "quake in the presence of God." Unlike the powerful Anglicans, Quakers believed that priests or other church officials were not necessary to help them experience God. The Quakers taught that every person could experience the "inner light" of God in his or her heart.

Because the Quakers refused to support the Anglican Church, they were persecuted by the English government. The English imprisoned about 15,000 Quakers between 1660 and 1680. Penn tried to change the government's policy by writing pamphlets supporting religious tolerance in England.

The English government ignored Penn's pleas for change. He soon realized that he might have to look for religious freedom elsewhere. Years earlier, Penn's father had loaned Charles II a large sum of money, which had not been repaid at the time of Admiral Penn's death. William Penn now asked Charles II to give him a large grant of land in North America as a way of paying off this **debt**.

"Penn's Woods"

In 1681, the king granted Penn's request. He gave Penn land in the New World and named the territory Pennsylvania, meaning "Penn's Woods." The land was about 48,000 square miles (124,800 square kilometers). It bordered the Delaware River and extended to a point 12 miles (19 kilometers) north of New Castle in Delaware.

Penn quickly realized that the land grant did not give his colony easy access to Delaware Bay and the Atlantic Ocean. Without such access, trade in his new colony would be difficult. In 1681, he wrote to his old family friend, the Duke of York, asking the duke if he would turn over his colony on the Delaware Bay to Penn. The duke agreed, giving Penn two more land grants. One was a 12-mile (19-kilometer) piece of land in a semicircle around New Castle. The second grant went southward to the entrance of the Delaware Bay.

The Lower Counties

The two new land grants became part of Pennsylvania. William Penn called this area along the Delaware River "the Lower Counties." It was divided into three counties named New Castle, Kent, and Sussex.

The government of Pennsylvania was made up of a council that advised the governor and a legislature. The

Lower Counties became part of Pennsylvania's government. Men from the Lower Counties were elected to help govern the colony. These men were called representatives. Penn believed strongly in religious freedom, not only for Quakers, but for other religious groups. Pennsylvania quickly became a **refuge** for settlers who wanted to escape religious persecution in Europe and practice their religion without fear. Some of them settled in the Lower Counties.

William Penn spoke to the Swedish colonists at New Castle, Delaware, and explained his charter from King Charles II.

Penn soon found himself in a conflict with Charles Calvert, also known as Lord Baltimore, over the ownership of the Lower Counties. Calvert had been given a land grant that became known as Maryland. Since the 1630s, when the land was first granted to the Calvert family, they had claimed that it included the Lower Counties near the Delaware River. In 1682, Penn traveled to Maryland to discuss this conflict with Lord Baltimore, but they were unable to come to any agreement.

The following year, Lord Baltimore sent his cousin, Captain George Talbot, north to build a small fort on the Christina River. Talbot told the settlers that they owed no **allegiance** to Pennsylvania.

Finally, in 1685, Penn, frustrated by these squabbles, sailed to England to speak directly with the king. By this time, King Charles had died and his brother, the Duke of York, was now King James II.

The king supported Penn's claim to the Lower Counties, saying that Lord Baltimore's grant only included land that had not already been settled. At the time of Lord Baltimore's grant, in the 1630s, the Dutch had already settled a colony along Delaware Bay, and so this area now remained a part of Pennsylvania.

Life in the Lower Counties

During the late seventeenth century, most of the settlers in the Lower Counties were farmers who grew corn and wheat. The early colonists used wooden plows, with iron plowshares (the part of the plow that cuts the earth), to prepare the soil to receive seeds. Farming was hard work. The farmer's day started at sunrise and ended at sunset. The whole family, including children, spent most of their time doing chores and working in order to grow enough to eat.

According to one settler, the colonists planted

3 sorts of Wheat, as Winter, Summer,
and Buck Wheat; the Winter Wheat they
sow at the fall, the Summer Wheat in March,
these two sorts are ripe in June; then having
taken in this, they plow the same land, and sow
Buck Wheat, which is ripe in September.

Once the wheat was ripe, the farmer cut it with a sickle, a small blade with a wooden handle, or a scythe, which had a larger, curved blade. The stalks were then bundled together, stacked, and taken to a barn with a wooden floor, where they were beaten with wooden sticks to knock the grain free. Finally, the grain was separated from the chaff (the seed coverings) by being poured from the upper level of the barn to the lower level on a windy day. The wind blew away the chaff, which was very light, and the heavier grain fell to the barn floor. Then the farm workers gathered the grain into sacks or barrels.

Corn was harvested late in the fall. At a cornhusking party around a bonfire, families peeled away the husk (outer covering) of the corn so it could be dried and stored for the winter. A red ear of corn was a symbol of good luck.

As winter set in, farmers slaughtered some of their hogs. The fat from the animals was turned into lard, used in cooking. Some of the meat became ham or bacon. Any meat that was not immediately eaten was salted and preserved to be used later in the winter.

In colonial households, women and their daughters took care of preparing the meals and making the clothes. They roasted meat over fire in the hearths (fireplaces) and baked bread made from wheat or corn. Women also grew flax and wove it into linen. Girls learned how to spin wool from the sheep raised on the family farm and how to sew it into warm clothing that could withstand the cold winds of winter.

Swedish farmers used sickles with curved blades to cut wheat.

Trade Goods

While much of the clothing and food produced by the settlers in the Lower Counties was for their own use, some of it was sold in the towns that developed along the Delaware River. New Castle became an important trading community where ships stopped on their way to and from Philadelphia, the capital of Pennsylvania. The merchants of New Castle also developed a brisk trade in meat and grain with English colonies in the Caribbean.

Tobacco, grown on Delaware's plantations, was also exported from New Castle. Tobacco seeds were planted in the spring and weeded during the summer. Some of the work was done by slaves brought over from Africa. By 1700, there were still fewer than 150 slaves in the Lower Counties. They often worked side by side in the fields with plantation owners and their families. Tobacco plants had to be carefully tended to make sure they were not attacked by caterpillars or worms that could destroy the leaves. In the fall, when the leaves turned yellow-green, they were picked, tied together, and dried in tobacco barns. Once dry, the tobacco was packed in barrels for shipment abroad.

Conflict with Philadelphia

As the settlements in the Lower Counties grew, they had many disagreements with the Pennsylvania government over the issue of how best to defend their colony. Quakers did not believe in making war for any reason. The Quaker leaders of Pennsylvania did not believe in carrying weapons. But the settlements of the Lower Counties lay along the Delaware Bay, which was open to attack by enemy ships.

In 1689, war broke out between England and the combined forces of France and Spain. The war was known as King William's War. The settlers in the Lower Counties were afraid that France and Spain would attack them.

Representatives of the Lower Counties who sat in the legislature wanted forts to be built along Delaware Bay to protect the settlers from attack. But the Quakers from Pennsylvania refused to set aside any money to build forts there. Finally, in 1690, the Lower Counties set up a colonial **militia** (an army of citizen soldiers) to protect themselves. This, too, was opposed by the Pennsylvania Quakers. To smooth things out between the Lower Counties and the Quaker members of the assembly, William Penn decided that there should now be two governors, one for Pennsylvania and another for the Lower Counties.

This decision did not put an end to the conflict. The Quakers still prevented the governor of the Lower Counties from establishing forts along Delaware Bay. As a result, the towns along the bay were defenseless. In 1698, the town of Lewes was attacked by pirates, who broke into the homes of the settlers and carried off jewelry, money, and clothing.

At Quaker meetings, members of the church, both men and women, spoke out about important issues. They opposed any form of violence, including arming the Delaware militia.

Pirates

As the seventeenth century came to a close, pirates became a big problem for the Lower Counties. During King William's War, which ended in 1697, the English found independent ship captains to attack French shipping. These captains, called **privateers**, were hired by one country to fight against another. When privateers hired by England attacked a French ship, they were free to keep whatever they could take from that ship. Some privateers for the English captured rich cargos.

Pirates were a threat to coastal towns in Delaware. They sailed their ships into the town's harbor, robbed the residents, and escaped back out to sea in their ships.

After the war ended, these sea captains were expected to stop their privateering. But some of these captains, having grown used to living off the freight they captured, refused to stop. Instead, they became pirates. They began to prey on any ship they saw, even those of the English.

Conflict Continues

In 1701, the Pennsylvania legislature was asked to grant aid to New York, which was forced to deal with attacks by the French. Together with their Indian allies, the French were attacking English settlements in the colonies.

The **delegates** from the Lower Counties were angry that the assembly would even consider a request from New York settlers for arms and aid when it had refused to secure Delaware Bay. The conflict grew heated. Penn was finally forced to make a compromise with the Lower County delegates. They were given the go-ahead to create their own assembly and pass their own laws, with the approval of the Pennsylvania governor.

In 1704, the Lower Counties elected representatives to their own assembly, which began making laws for the settlers. This change brought a large amount of independence to Delaware, which it would enjoy for the remainder of the colonial era. This was Delaware's first step toward becoming an **independent** colony.

Even though most colonists had to work long hours to survive, they still found time to have fun. Colonial children and adults enjoyed many different games and toys. Some of their games, such as cards, chess, checkers, and dominoes, are still played today.

☞ In colonial times, many toys were made from wood. A rocking horse like this one took many hours to chisel and shape by hand.

☞ Colonial kites were made from paper, sticks, and string, just as they are today.

⚘ Ice-skating was a popular winter pastime in the northern colonies.

☞ Wooden tops were a favorite colonial toy.

58

Games

Many colonial families played card games. These playing cards from the 1700s are similar to those used today.

This elaborate game table might have been found in the home of a well-to-do colonial family.

Dominoes were carved from animal bone instead of being made of plastic.

Boys and girls rolled hoops made of metal or wood. It took skill to keep the hoop rolling along the ground.

CHAPTER FIVE

The Growth of the Colony

Willington

Throughout the eighteenth century, the Lower Counties continued to grow. More settlers arrived, establishing new communities. In 1727, a Swedish colonist named Andrew Jutison purchased a large parcel of land along the Christina River. Along with his son-in-law, a merchant named Thomas Willing, he began developing a new village, which they called Willington.

Ten years later, there were twenty additional homes in Willington, along with Willing's house on King Street. Willington was an excellent location for a new town, because it was right on the Christina River and also near the Brandywine Creek, which flowed into the Delaware.

The Old Dutch House in New Castle, Delaware, is a state landmark that has been standing since at least 1704.

Settlers whose farms lay along the rivers could easily load their corn and grain onto boats and ship their produce directly to Willington. From there, it was transported to England, to English colonies in the Caribbean, or to Philadelphia, which was rapidly becoming the largest city in North America. At the same time that Willington was being developed, a young woman in Philadelphia named Elizabeth Levis Shipley had a dream about the new village. Although she didn't know it at the time, this dream would play a large role in shaping Willington's future.

Elizabeth Shipley

More than any other religious group, the Quakers believed in equality between men and women. In most other religions, for example, women were not permitted to become priests or ministers and did not share equally in the running of the church.

Elizabeth Shipley was a Quaker preacher. She traveled to New England and the South to speak at meetings of the Society of Friends. In her dream, Shipley and a companion rode to the top of a hill and saw a new village. Shipley believed that God was directing her to move to this village and establish her home there.

Upon rising, Elizabeth told her husband, William, about the exciting dream. She was eager to look for the village.

Quaker ministers like Elizabeth Shipley traveled to Quaker meeting-houses and preached using both words and body movements.

William, however, was a successful merchant in Philadelphia. He made it clear that he had no intention of leaving the city to search for a new place to live.

Several years later, Elizabeth Shipley happened to pass through Willington on her way to preach at a Quaker meeting. She instantly recognized the village from her dream. Excited, she returned home and managed to persuade her husband to at least come and see the village. Upon seeing Willington's location near three rivers, William Shipley quickly recognized the possibilities for trading there and agreed to move. He not only built a house for Elizabeth and himself, but constructed a brewery and a wharf on the river. He also set up a private market on his own land, where farmers could sell their produce.

Other residents of Willington protested, believing that this newcomer was trying to corner the local trade. Banding together, other farmers and merchants built their own market on land provided by Willing. Willington's importance as a center of trade and shipping grew as a result of these competing markets.

By this time, the name of the town had been changed from Willington to Wilmington. In 1739, the Pennsylvania government, which still controlled the Lower Counties, had decided to rename the town after a friend of the Penn family, Spencer Compton, the Earl of Wilmington.

Quakers in the Lower Counties

The Lower Counties continued to grow during the 1740s. Many Quaker families arrived and built homes, laid out farms, and established meetinghouses where they practiced their religion. The Quakers built their homes in a distinctive style, with walls made out of local fieldstone, slate roofs, and white wood trim. Each house had several fireplaces and

Quaker Meetings

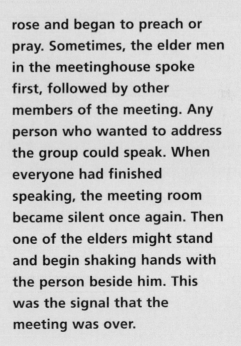

Members of the Society of Friends met in simple meeting-houses once a week or more. The houses were built of field-stone, with large windows and white shutters. Men and women did not enter a meet-inghouse together, but came in through separate doors, filing to the front until all the benches were filled.

As the meeting began, Friends sat quietly, waiting for God's inner light to fill their hearts. Eventually, individual Quakers rose and began to preach or pray. Sometimes, the elder men in the meetinghouse spoke first, followed by other members of the meeting. Any person who wanted to address the group could speak. When everyone had finished speaking, the meeting room became silent once again. Then one of the elders might stand and begin shaking hands with the person beside him. This was the signal that the meeting was over.

The old meetinghouse at Chester, Pennsylvania, was the home of William Penn and an example of a typical Quaker home from the seventeenth and eighteenth centuries.

chimneys, as well as a corner stairway to connect the first and second floors. Small wooden coverings, called pent roofs, which offered protection from rain and snow, were built over doorways and supported by thin wooden pillars.

The Quakers believed in a simple lifestyle. Rich carpets on the floors, paintings on the walls, and fancy decorations of any kind were considered much too showy for Quaker homes. Their furniture was practical, consisting of only a few chairs and a table in the dining room, stools and a long bench in the **parlor**, and beds and benches in the bedrooms. Meals were prepared in the kitchens, which had large fireplaces for baking and roasting.

Most Quaker farmers ate their largest meal during the middle of the day, which gave them energy to work in the fields. They had only a light meal in the evening, because they often went to bed soon after sunset. Quakers also dressed simply, never wearing fancy clothes. Men wore gray jackets and pants with broad-brimmed hats, and women wore gray dresses. Out in public, women also wore green or blue aprons.

The Quaker Family

Life in Quaker families differed from that of other families in colonial America. During the eighteenth century, the husband or father in most families was considered to be the person in charge. His word was final, with no discussion or argument permitted. Children often lived in fear of punishment from their father if they disobeyed him.

However, in Quaker families, there was far more equality between husbands and wives. In non-Quaker families, children referred to their homes as "my father's house." According to historian David Hackett Fischer, Quaker children called their homes "my father and mother's house." Quaker parents also allowed their children more freedom. Children could disagree with their parents without being punished. Quakers believed strongly in rewarding their children for good behavior instead of punishing them for wrongdoing.

Of course, this did not mean that Quaker children could simply do as they pleased. Quaker girls were expected to learn how to do household chores, like cooking, sewing, and cleaning, while boys were supposed to work alongside their fathers in the fields.

In addition, education was very important to the Quakers. No matter how busy children were with chores, their parents also made sure that they had time for learning.

Quaker Words

The Quakers introduced many words and phrases to the Delaware Valley. Among them are the following.

Term	Meaning
apple-pie order	neat and tidy
to bamboozle	to lie and cheat
blather	meaningless talk
to budge	to move
chock-full	entirely full
dresser	chest of drawers
to knuckle under	to give in
rumpus	noise
tiff	disagreement

School was held in local Quaker meetinghouses, where children learned to read and write. They were also taught the importance of community service. Quakers believed strongly that everyone had a responsibility to help others who were less fortunate.

In addition to attending school and doing chores, some Quaker children also served apprenticeships with local artisans. A child would live with a carpenter or blacksmith in Wilmington or travel to Philadelphia to learn a valuable trade.

Immigrants to the Lower Counties

In addition to the Quakers, other groups began moving to the Lower Counties. Between 1700 and 1760, the colony grew from 3,000 to 35,000 people. Among the new settlers were people originally from Scotland who had lived in Ireland for years. In Ireland, they worked farms owned by English landlords. These people were known as the Scotch-Irish.

The Scotch-Irish had lived in poor conditions in Ireland. Their English landlords regularly raised the rents that the Scotch-Irish were required to pay. The Scotch-Irish were also forced to give money to support the Anglican Church, although most of them were not Anglicans themselves, but Presbyterians. This religion was founded in the sixteenth century in Switzerland.

To escape the conditions in Ireland, the Scotch-Irish began coming to North America during the eighteenth century. Since many of them were poor, they often came as indentured servants, who agreed to work for someone who would pay for their transport.

Ship captains agreed to take these immigrants to North America. When they arrived at Wilmington or New Castle, the captains sold the indentured servants to local farmers. The new immigrants then agreed to work for these farmers as servants. They usually had to work for five to seven years, until they paid off what the farmers had paid to hire them. When their time was up, indentured servants were free to start their own businesses. Some masters gave their indentured servants money or tools to help them get started in their new lives. Because of the religious freedom in the Lower Counties, the Scotch-Irish were able to establish their own Presbyterian churches. Presbyterian ministers, in turn, set up local schools.

Other immigrant groups, such as the Germans and the Welsh, came to the Lower Counties as well. The Lower Counties also attracted settlers from nearby colonies. In the 1740s, many tobacco and wheat farmers left Maryland to move to the Lower Counties. Farming on the same land over and over had ruined the soil on their farms. They came in search of fertile land.

Indentured servants had to work for Delaware farmers for five to seven years in order to earn their freedom.

Slavery in the Lower Counties

Some of the tobacco farmers who **migrated** from Maryland brought their slaves with them. By 1750, about 1,500 slaves lived in the Lower Counties, making up about 5 percent of the total population. This was a small number of slaves compared to the number in colonies such as Virginia or South Carolina. Slaves were captured in Africa, usually by local tribes who kidnapped men, women, and children from their villages. The slaves were then chained together and taken to the western coast of Africa. There, they were sold to European slave traders.

Africans were captured in their homelands by slavers and brought to the coast, where they were sold to slave traders.

The slaves were then loaded into cramped quarters below the decks of small sailing ships. During the day, the slaves were brought above deck to be fed. The crew also forced the slaves to dance to keep their bodies limber. The slaves suffered from seasickness and many serious diseases during rough voyages across the Atlantic. Many died before arriving in North America.

A Slave's Life

Some slave ships sailed to Philadelphia, where the slaves were sold to local farmers. A few slaves were also transported to the Lower Counties. Farmers there usually owned just a few slaves to help them in the fields, while other slaves worked for artisans, such as carpenters and blacksmiths. The slaves generally lived in the same houses as their masters.

Some slaves married and raised families in the Delaware Valley. But a husband and wife might be split up when one was sold to a different master. If they still lived close to each other, the male slave might receive permission to visit his wife and children for twenty-four hours. This usually occurred on Sundays, which was a day of rest in the colonies. This separation created an enormous hardship for slave families. Even worse, a slave might be sold to a master who lived far away. Slaves who were moved to a distant farm might never see their family again.

Rules for Slaves

Although there was never a large number of slaves in the Lower Counties, white settlers still worried about the possibility of a slave revolt. In 1739, a revolt had occurred in South Carolina, where a small army of about a hundred slaves had risen up and killed white settlers before being captured by the local militia.

To prevent anything like that from happening in the Lower Counties, local leaders passed a series of laws. For example, slaves were not permitted to carry weapons or meet together in large groups. Some of the settlers in the Lower Counties thought that these laws were unfair. Quakers, for example, believed that all people were equal in the sight of God, no matter what race they were. The Quakers wanted slavery **abolished**, and they urged any member of their religion who owned slaves to free them. Because of this, a number of freed slaves lived in New Castle, Kent, and Sussex counties, where they worked as farmers and artisans.

The Growth of Industry

New industry sprang up along the rivers of the Lower Counties during the eighteenth century, strengthening the economy of the colony. North of Wilmington, the

This colonial farm has a water-powered mill for grinding wheat and other grains into flour.

Brandywine Creek raced over rapids and tumbled down waterfalls, creating a natural source of waterpower. Local settlers harnessed the power of rushing water by building a narrow channel, or raceway, and then funneling the flowing water through it into small mills.

In a mill, the powerful movement of the water turned a wooden wheel that was connected by gears to two huge millstones. Each millstone was about 4 feet (1.2 meters) across and made from pieces of granite held together by metal braces. As the stones turned, grains of wheat were poured between the two stones and ground into flour.

Paying the Miller

Delaware was known for its grain and lumber mills. The people who ran the mills were called millers. Often a husband and wife ran the mill together. Milling was hard work. The grain or lumber had to be stored and then carried to the mill to be ground or cut.

When a farmer brought grain or wood to the mill, he had to pay the miller for the work. Most farmers paid the miller with a portion of the finished product. This was a form of barter (trading goods without using money).

The flour or meal (coarsely ground grain) and finished boards were valuable. The miller could easily trade them for things like food, gunpowder, and even services like shoeing horses.

Mills sprang up in towns that were given names like Millville and Milford. From these mills, flour was shipped down the Delaware River to ports in Europe and the Caribbean.

In addition to flour mills, the settlers of the Lower Counties also opened lumber mills and tanneries. Trees taken from the forest were brought to the lumber mills and cut into boards, again using water-powered equipment. These boards were then used to build houses and ships. Animal hides were shipped to tanneries along the Delaware River. There, the hides were first cleaned and soaked in limewater to soften them. Then they were treated with tannic acid to prevent them from rotting. Tannic acid was removed from the bark of oak and hemlock trees. The hides were cured (soaked) in a series of pits, each of which had a stronger and stronger mix of tannic acid and water. Afterward, the hides were dried and oiled. The result was a tough leather that could be made into shoes and other items.

Religious Revival

Industry was growing in the Lower Counties. Religious belief was, too. In October 1739, an English minister named George Whitefield arrived in the town of Lewes. Whitefield was a spellbinding Methodist preacher who attracted large crowds to his fiery worship services. He presented an impassioned, lively approach to religion, pleading with his listeners to get in touch with God. He lured them away from other religious leaders, who he believed were cold and uninteresting.

Whitefield made several trips to North America over the next two decades, carrying his message up and down the Atlantic seaboard. He added many new members to his Methodist church. As many colonists embraced a newfound **spirituality,** however, a bloody conflict arose that threatened the very existence of the English settlements.

CHAPTER SIX

Delaware in the Colonial Wars

Attacks by the French

During the course of the eighteenth century, England and France fought a series of wars for control of North America. Both nations had established valuable colonies in the New World. Now each wanted complete control of the region. The settlers of Delaware were greatly involved in these wars.

The French had built settlements in New France along the St. Lawrence River. They controlled parts of the Mississippi River and the Great Lakes. From these outposts, the French carried on a fur trade with the Indian

During the 1600s, French trappers and explorers made friends with the Indian tribes who lived north and west of Delaware and the other English colonies. The Indians became allies of the French and fought against the English colonists.

tribes of the region. The French formed strong alliances with the Indians. With their help, the French hoped to keep the English in their narrow strip of settlements along the Atlantic coast.

The French wanted to prevent English settlers from expanding westward. With their Indian allies, the French regularly raided settlements on the western **frontiers** of New England, New York, and Pennsylvania. The raiding parties of French and Indians attacked English farms, killing entire families and burning their homes. The raiders also kidnapped townspeople and carried them off to Indian villages.

Because of their location, the Lower Counties were protected from most attacks by the French. However, in 1709, the town of Lewes was attacked twice by the French and their Indian allies. These attacks were part of France's policy of protecting its own settlements. As one French leader put it, "[We should prepare ourselves] in a way to stop the English, who have long tried to seize French America."

Battles between England and its enemies, France and Spain, continued for years. On July 12, 1747, a small expedition of French and Spanish soldiers appeared in Delaware Bay. They attacked several plantations in the Lower Counties and captured a ship near Cape Henlopen. Two months later, a French privateer sailed into Delaware Bay and captured two merchant ships. Desperate for stronger

Indians working with the French raided farms and settlements throughout the western frontier of Delaware.

defenses, colonial leaders added cannons at Wilmington to protect the town against future attacks. Defenses were also strengthened at New Castle.

In 1748, France and England signed a treaty ending their current war. But this treaty provided only a short period of peace before the final war between the two nations. The future of North America hung in the balance.

A young soldier named George Washington traveled to the Ohio River valley to deliver a message to the French commander there.

The French and Indian War

The peace that followed the battles between the French and English would last only a few years. Both countries wanted to control the fur trade in North America. They both claimed a large territory called the Ohio River valley northwest of Delaware. Battles for this territory would start a seven-year war that would decide the fate of North America.

Both French and English traders lived among the Indian tribes of the valley, and each side tried to win the loyalty of the natives. The English tried to offer the Indians better prices than the French for furs. The English also gave the Indians more gifts and sold them gunpowder and muskets.

Finally, in the early 1750s, the French governor of New France, Marquis Duquesne, decided to drive the English from the Ohio Valley. In 1753, he sent a force south from New France to strengthen the area.

Virginia and Pennsylvania wanted to settle the area themselves. They did not like having French troops so close to their borders. In the winter of 1753, Virginia's governor, Robert Dinwiddie, sent a small expedition to warn the French to leave the valley. After traveling through snow and freezing rain, the expedition finally reached a French stronghold in the Ohio Valley. A tall Virginian named George Washington approached the wooden stockade (wall) that surrounded the fort. He read aloud a letter for the French commander, written by Governor Dinwiddie:

I must desire you to acquaint me by whose authority and instructions you have lately marched from Canada with an armed force, and invaded the King of Great Britain's territories. It becomes my duty to require your peaceable departure.

The French commander was very polite to Lieutenant Washington and his companions. However, he made it clear that the French would not leave the Ohio Valley.

The following year, the French built a new fort called Fort Duquesne along the Ohio River. Washington led a small force of men into the Ohio Valley to attempt to drive off the French, but he was defeated. This battle was small, but it had the effect of starting the French and Indian War.

More Battles

One year after Washington's defeat, England sent an army to North America to recapture territory that had been lost to the French. In February 1755, General Edward Braddock arrived in Virginia with two companies of English soldiers. At Alexandria, Braddock met with several of the colonial governors. He outlined a plan of attack against the French. Part of the plan called for Braddock to march westward and capture Fort Duquesne from the French.

Joining Braddock's troops were colonial militia from Virginia, Maryland, and North Carolina. Although the Lower Counties sent no soldiers, they did send supplies to Braddock's army—a herd of cattle, hams, cheeses, fish, biscuits, and potatoes.

By early July, Braddock had cut a road through the forest that brought his army within 10 miles (16 kilometers) of Fort Duquesne. As the English approached, the French sent out a force of about 900 soldiers and Indians who ambushed

The British general Edward Braddock suffered a major defeat at Fort Duquesne at the beginning of the French and Indian War.

Braddock's troops. Hundreds of British soldiers were hit by musket fire, including Braddock himself. The general fell from his horse and later died. The English soldiers fled from the battlefield eastward to Williamsburg, Virginia. Newspapers describing this terrible disaster reached the Lower Counties a few weeks later. The colony did not publish its own newspaper, but many colonists read the *Pennsylvania Gazette*, which was printed in Philadelphia.

For the next three years, the English frontier was constantly attacked by the French and their Indian allies. During this time, a settler could go out hunting deer to provide food for the family, only to return home and find the house burned to the ground and the family killed.

The Capture of Fort Duquesne

The British were outraged by these attacks. In 1758, they launched another assault on Fort Duquesne. They thought this fort was a key to controlling the Ohio River valley. This attack, led by General John Forbes, included British regular troops as well as militia from Virginia, Maryland, North Carolina, and the Lower Counties.

Forbes built a road for his army from Pennsylvania to the Ohio River. Three hundred militiamen from the Lower Counties helped cut the trees, remove the boulders, and build bridges across the rivers on the way to Fort Duquesne.

Lower Counties Militia

The Native Americans planted corn, beans, and squash in a specific pattern called "the Three Sisters." This grouping, which was helpful to all three plants, showed how the woodland Indians understood their environment.

Beans grow on vine-like stems, which need to wrap themselves around poles. Cornstalks grow tall, providing perfect poles for the bean stems. Beans also make the soil richer as they grow. Squash grows low to the ground and produces large, flat leaves. These leaves protect the bases of all three plants, keeping weeds down and helping the soil to stay moist.

During this time, the French position on the Ohio River had been weakened. The Indians in the Ohio Valley had signed a peace treaty with the English, who promised to respect their lands. As the English marched closer to Fort Duquesne, the French realized that they did not have the ability to defend it. Rather than surrender the fort, they blew it up and retreated north to New France.

Strengthened by this victory, the English invaded Canada. Eventually, they captured the French strongholds of Quebec and Montreal. England now had control of a vast North American empire. But this victory came with a price. Paying the price would create new problems for England, the Lower Counties, and the other English colonies in North America. It would also lead to the creation of new nation.

CHAPTER SEVEN

The Coming of Revolution

New Taxes

The French and Indian War finally ended. In 1763, in the Treaty of Paris, France formally handed over its large empire in New France to England. The English gave New France a new name—Canada. This British victory took away one threat to the North American colonies. But it brought with it another set of difficulties that sparked a revolution.

The French and Indian War had been very expensive, forcing Great Britain to run up huge debts. To add to their money problems, the English also had to hold a chain of military posts on the western frontier of their colonies.

Colonists in Delaware and the other colonies became very unhappy with British taxes in the mid-1700s. The taxes resulted in many protests and eventually led the colonies to declare their independence from England.

This was because the Indian tribes who were friends with the French still remained hostile to English settlers. These forts were very costly to keep up. The British needed a way to pay the cost of these posts and the debts from the war. So the British Parliament, the main governing body in England, decided to tax the American colonies.

In 1765, Parliament passed the first of a series of taxes to be paid by the people in the colonies. The first new tax was called the Stamp Act. It required colonists to pay for a stamp that had to appear on all printed material. This included newspapers, marriage certificates, court documents, and even the papers that ships needed to enter harbors in North America.

Many colonists opposed the tax. They argued that the colonies' governments had also gone into debt to defend themselves during the French and Indian War. The colonists said that they could not afford to pay extra any more than the British could.

Led by Massachusetts, the colonists agreed to hold a Stamp Act Congress in New York during the fall of 1765 to  discuss this tax. Along with other colonies, the Lower Counties appointed delegates to the congress, including Caesar Rodney of Kent County and Thomas McKean of New Castle County.

The Stamp Act caused widespread protests. Crowds of angry Patriots rioted in the streets.

At the congress, Rodney and McKean, along with representatives from other colonies, called on the British Parliament to repeal, or end, the Stamp Act. They said that Great Britain had no right to tax the colonies because the colonies had no way to speak for themselves in Parliament. The phrase "no taxation without representation" would become a rallying cry of the Revolutionary War.

The Stamp Act Congress sent word to England of its demand. Meanwhile, protests against the tax were held in the Lower Counties. In the port town of Lewes, a crowd stopped officials from collecting the tax on incoming ships. The Lower Counties and the other colonies also decided to stop buying English goods as a way of putting pressure on Parliament. This **boycott** badly hurt British merchants, who finally convinced Parliament to repeal the Stamp Act.

More Taxes

The colonists were relieved after the repeal of the Stamp Tax, but a year later, in 1766, Parliament imposed more taxes, called the Townshend Acts. Named after Charles Townshend, the head of England's treasury, these acts taxed certain goods, such as paint, glass, paper, and tea, which were exported from England to the colonies.

At a meeting, McKean, Rodney, and George Read, another member of the Delaware assembly, prepared a document stating that the colonies were once again being taxed without their approval or representation. The colonies once again refused to import English goods. But this time, not all settlers of the Lower Counties supported the boycott. At first, some merchants continued to make money by trading with the British. Read had to urge them to follow the other colonies and stop this trade.

Tea and Revolution

Three years later, Parliament passed the Tea Act, which made the British East India Company the only company allowed to sell tea in the colonies without a tax. The act led to large, angry protests in many of the colonies. In December

A group of Patriots called the Sons of Liberty dressed as Indians and threw large bales of tea from British ships into Boston Harbor.

1773, Boston Patriots (people opposed to English rule) disguised as Indians boarded English ships. They threw large boxes of tea belonging to the East India Company into the harbor in what became known as the Boston Tea Party.

After the Boston Tea Party, the English navy shut down the port of Boston. This cut off supplies to the colony, putting the livelihoods of many merchants, sailors, and local shop owners at risk. Throughout the colonies, loud protests sounded against the British action in Boston. In the Lower Counties, colonists held meetings where they spoke out against the English king and Parliament.

In 1774, the Lower Counties Assembly selected delegates to attend the First Continental Congress. The congress was to be held at Carpenter's Hall in Philadelphia. It would be made up of representatives from all the colonies. The delegates were going to discuss what to do in response to the taxes being demanded by Parliament. Many delegates believed that the time for revolution was near.

Caesar Rodney, Thomas McKean, and George Read were selected to represent the Lower Counties at the congress. Several hundred delegates argued for seven weeks about how to respond to Parliament. They finally decided to send letters to England. These letters would oppose the action taken in Boston Harbor. The delegates also decided to start another boycott of English goods and to meet again

British troops fought against Patriot militiamen in Lexington, Massachusetts, in the first battle of the Revolutionary War.

in 1775. At this Second Continental Congress, they would follow up on their letters.

By the time that second meeting took place, however, war had already broken out in Massachusetts. On April 19, 1775, British soldiers stationed in Boston were sent to two towns nearby. Their mission was to capture leading colonial Patriots and the Patriots' supply of gunpowder. Along the way, the British clashed with members of the Massachusetts militia at battles in Lexington and Concord. These were the first battles of the Revolutionary War.

The Lower Counties
Prepare for War

The Lower Counties began gathering militia units to defend the colony. The militia units were formed under the direction of a group called the Council of Safety. At the same time, Rodney, Read, and McKean returned to Philadelphia to attend the Second Continental Congress.

Letters from a Pennsylvania Farmer

During the argument over the Townshend Acts, another political leader with Delaware roots, John Dickinson, became famous for writing his *Letters from a Pennsylvania Farmer.* Dickinson's father Samuel had purchased a plantation in Kent County and moved his family there when John was eight years old.

In 1760, John Dickinson was elected to the Lower Counties Assembly. His *Letters* were read throughout the colonies and in Europe. In them, he argued that taxing the colonies without their consent was unreasonable. He said that the taxes were opposed to the spirit of English laws. But it was the colonial boycott of English goods more than Dickinson's words that finally convinced Parliament to repeal the Townshend Acts in 1770.

In the spring of 1775, during the early stages of the congress, the delegates sent King George III a letter. This document was written by John Dickinson. It was called the Olive Branch Petition (an olive branch is a traditional symbol of peace). The petition called for a peaceful solution to the situation if Parliament and the king changed their policies. Many people in the Lower Counties agreed with the principles of the Olive Branch Petition. These people hoped that full-scale war might be avoided. However, King George III rejected this petition.

Meanwhile, the Congress created a continental army for the colonies. The army formed outside Boston and attacked British soldiers stationed inside the city. In the Lower Counties, the Council of Safety began raising troops for the Continental army. But some residents of the colony did not want to wait for their own company of troops to be formed. Some went south to fight in Virginia, where fighting between colonists and British soldiers had already begun. Others joined an American army force that invaded Canada and attacked Quebec during a driving snowstorm. For the people of the Lower Counties, the Revolutionary War had begun. Eight years of pain and bloodshed would follow.

CHAPTER EIGHT

Independence and Statehood

Debating Independence

The spirit of revolution filled Independence Hall in Philadelphia where the Second Continental Congress was meeting. On June 7, 1776, Richard Henry Lee of Virginia read a resolution stating that

> *these United Colonies are and of right,*
> *ought to be, free and independent states,*
> *that they are absolved from all allegiance to*
> *the British Crown, and that all political connection*
> *between them and the State of Great Britain,*
> *is and ought to be, totally dissolved.*

⌐ Crowds gathered outside Independence Hall in Philadelphia, Pennsylvania, as the Declaration of Independence was read aloud.

The bold resolution called for the colonies to break free from the grasp of England. It was considered and debated by the delegates throughout June. A vote was finally taken on July 1. Nine colonies supported the resolution, while four others were either opposed or undecided. The Lower Counties were undecided.

Of the three Lower Counties delegates, Thomas McKean supported independence, but George Read was against it. These delegates demonstrated the divided feelings among the colonists of the Lower Counties. Some favored independence. Others still wanted to remain a part of the British Empire, even though they did not like the harsh British taxes. The third member of the Lower Counties delegation, Caesar Rodney, was back in New Castle, carrying out his duties as speaker of the assembly. Rodney favored independence.

The delegation from each colony had to vote as a single unit. Further, a majority of the Lower Counties delegates was needed in order to come to a decision. Although nine colonies had voted in favor of independence, all the delegates at the congress wanted a **unanimous** vote before declaring themselves free from England. Otherwise, they feared, conflicts among the colonies would weaken them while they were fighting a war against Great Britain.

Rodney's Ride

Another vote on independence was scheduled for July 2. McKean sent a message to New Castle, telling Rodney to go to Philadelphia to vote. It was an 80-mile (128-kilometer) trip on horseback during hot summer weather.

Rodney raced northward through Wilmington, braving heavy rains, thunder, and lightning. The final vote had been postponed until the afternoon of July 2. Rodney rode down the cobbled streets of Philadelphia and finally arrived at Independence Hall just as the delegates were completing

Caesar Rodney rode through foul weather to Philadelphia to cast his vote supporting independence.

their debates. He entered the meeting room exhausted and caked with mud.

When the vote was finally taken, two of the states that had been opposed or undecided before now supported independence. New York **abstained**, choosing not to vote at all. With Rodney now present at the convention to add his "yes" vote to McKean's, the Lower Counties voted to support independence. When the Declaration of Independence was finally issued, on July 4, it was signed by all three delegates from the Lower Counties. George Read had agreed to go along with the decision of the others.

The united colonies, now calling themselves the United States, had declared that they were no longer colonies. They were now free states and part of a free nation. England would see them differently.

The New State of Delaware and Its Soldiers

After the vote for independence, an election was held in the Lower Counties. This election was to choose representatives for a statewide constitutional convention. This meeting was held at New Castle in August. Its purpose was to create a new constitution for the Lower Counties, which were now calling themselves the state of Delaware.

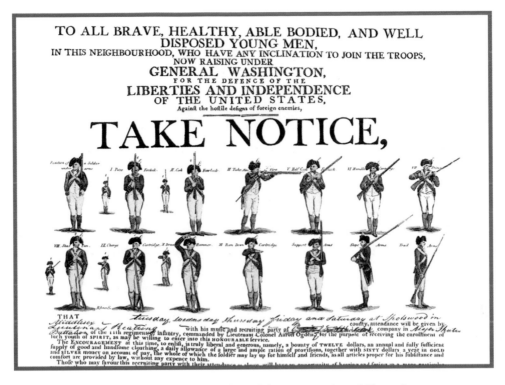

The Patriot army used posters like this to recruit soldiers from Delaware and the other colonies to fight against the British.

While Delaware was busy creating a new state government, the Continental army of the United States, including soldiers from Delaware, was already battling British troops to the north. In August, a British army, commanded by General William Howe, met the Continentals, at the Battle of Long Island, near New York City. The Continentals were led by General George Washington.

A Delaware regiment was sent to join Washington. The Delaware soldiers wore blue coats with **buckskin** pants and small, black leather hats. Although the Continental troops put up a good fight, they were greatly outnumbered.

Both the British and American armies used cannons, which were called artillery, to blast the opposing side.

The Americans were forced to retreat. Washington was driven out of New York, which was then occupied by the British.

After taking control of New York City, the British went north to the town of White Plains, New York. White Plains was defended by the Continental army. The Delaware troops, under Colonel John Haslet, took up a position at Chatterton Hill. The British army arrived, cannons blazing, and began shelling the hill. As Haslet put it, the British **artillery** "kept up a continual peal of...thunder."

To answer this attack, Colonel Haslet ordered his own artillery to fire at the British. With drums beating, the redcoats (British soldiers) advanced. They held muskets with bayonets (sharp blades) of shining steel attached to the ends. When some of the American soldiers saw the English bayonets coming toward them, they broke ranks and fled. At first, the Delaware troops held their position, but they were eventually overcome by the enormous British attack. "Seeing ourselves deserted on all hands," Haslet later wrote, "and the continued column of the enemy advancing, we…retired."

Washington's army left New York and retreated through New Jersey. The Delaware troops acted as the rear guard to beat back any attack by the British. By December, the Continental army had crossed the Delaware River into Pennsylvania. There, it would spend a long, bitter winter.

Delaware Soldiers Fight the British

While Washington's army remained in Pennsylvania, the British occupied New Jersey. For the Americans, the war had reached an important stage. Their revolution was in danger of being quickly crushed by the British. Soldiers from Delaware, however, would soon help General Washington. Washington had given up New York, lost New Jersey, and retreated across the Delaware River with an army of only about 5,000 men. The Continental soldiers were poorly equipped to survive the harsh winter. They did not have warm clothing. Many of them marched without shoes. In addition, they had very little ammunition.

It appeared that Washington could do nothing to stop the British if they decided to cross the Delaware River and attack. But armies at that time usually did not fight during the winter months, due to the harsh weather. General Howe was not going to attack right away. Instead, the British commander put his soldiers into winter quarters, a series of posts from New York to the Delaware River, to wait for spring. At Trenton, New Jersey, he stationed a force of Hessians, German soldiers who were **allied** with the British.

Washington realized that to raise his troops' spirits and save the cause of American independence, he needed a quick victory against the enemy. Gathering a fleet of small boats, he decided to cross the Delaware River and surprise the Hessians on Christmas night. He expected that the German soldiers would be celebrating the holiday and therefore would not be ready to fight.

In a driving storm of snow and freezing rain, the Continental army, including Haslet's Delaware troops, crossed the Delaware River in darkness. Then the army marched on Trenton before eight o'clock in the morning. The surprised Hessians sleepily rolled out of their beds and unsuccessfully tried to fight off the Americans.

The Germans were overpowered. Their commander, Colonel Johann Rall, was seriously wounded. He quickly surrendered his army. With this victory at Trenton and another triumph a week later at Princeton, New Jersey, Washington kept the spirit of independence alive.

George Washington loaded his troops into small boats and crossed the Delaware River to fight the British forces at Trenton, New Jersey.

War Comes to Delaware

Spring finally arrived. General Howe now had a plan to attack the American capital at Philadelphia. Howe hoped that its capture would force the Americans to make peace with Great Britain. This plan brought the war to Delaware. By July, Howe had gathered a large fleet of more than 260 ships and as many as 18,000 troops. Leaving New York, he sailed for Chesapeake Bay. Howe planned to sail up the Chesapeake to its head and then march inland toward Philadelphia.

The British arrived at the head of the Chesapeake near the end of August and started marching north. As the British moved toward Philadelphia, Washington's army took up a defensive position on Brandywine Creek, south of the city. The Delaware soldiers were stationed along the river.

When the battle began, part of the British army attacked Washington's troops from the front. The rest of the redcoats tried to get behind the Americans. The Delaware troops moved from their position along the river to confront the British. The British unleashed their cannons against the Americans. As one captain from Delaware put it, "Cannon balls flew thick and many and small arms [musket fire] roared like the rolling of a drum." The Americans were greatly outnumbered and soon forced to retreat. The day

At first, the American army held its ground at the Battle of the Brandywine. But British cannon fire soon forced it to retreat.

after the battle at the Brandywine, the British captured Wilmington. General Howe's army then marched toward Philadelphia and captured it about two weeks later.

The British Hold Philadelphia

For the next five weeks, the British sent their sick and wounded to the hospital at Wilmington. With the British also holding nearby Philadelphia and patrolling Chesapeake Bay, tension grew between Patriots and Tories in Delaware. (Tories were those still loyal to the British government.)

Delaware Tories were supplying British sailors on Chesapeake Bay with cattle, flour, and vegetables. Caesar Rodney, who was a general in the American army, arrested some of these Tories. He put them in a prison in Dover, Delaware.

In the spring of 1778, the British decided to leave Philadelphia. Howe had hoped that his capture of the city might end the war. But the Continental Congress, which was in charge of the American war effort, had left Philadelphia before Howe entered it. The congress continued to carry on the war from York, Pennsylvania. Howe marched his troops across New Jersey and returned to New York. The focus of the Revolutionary War now shifted to the colonies in the South.

Delaware Troops in the Southern Campaigns

Loyal Delaware troops traveled far from home to continue fighting the British in the South. They participated in several battles that proved key to the final American victory. By early 1779, the British had captured Savannah and Augusta, Georgia, taking over the entire state.

During the fall of that year, British generals Henry Clinton and Charles Cornwallis led an army of 8,500 soldiers in an attack on Charles Town, South Carolina. The American forces were trapped inside Charles Town and forced to surrender. From this strong position, General Cornwallis sent troops into South Carolina. He soon controlled much of the state.

The Americans hoped to stop the number of British victories in the South. American forces under the command of General Horatio Gates tried to beat back the redcoats, attacking them at Camden, South Carolina. Battle-hardened Delaware and Maryland troops joined with inexperienced members of the North Carolina and Virginia militias.

Blue Hen's Chickens

The bravery of the Delaware soldiers during the American Revolution was often compared to the courage of a special type of fighting rooster. This bird was known as a "Blue Hen's Chicken," because it was the offspring of a bluish hen. As a result, the Delaware regiment became known as "the Blue Hen's Chickens." Later, the people of the state were given the same nickname.

The British, under General Cornwallis, fired a **volley** from their muskets against the militias. Then the British advanced with their bayonets. Seeing the scarlet coats and the glittering steel of the bayonets coming toward them, the militia soldiers ran from the field. The Delaware troops fought bravely. But they were soon surrounded and forced to surrender.

More Battles in the South

Under General Daniel Morgan, the Delaware soldiers and other American troops then took up a position at Cowpens, South Carolina, in January 1781. They awaited an attack by British troops under the command of Colonel Banastre Tarleton. The Delaware troops were placed in Morgan's main line, with the local militia a short distance in front of them.

When the British appeared, the militia fired only a couple of volleys, then fell back. Seeing this, Tarleton's troops advanced, believing they were overpowering the Continental army. Suddenly, the redcoats were met by a

massive musket volley from the American main line. In a few minutes, the battle was over. The Continental army, with men from Delaware on the front line, had won a tremendous victory.

After the battle at Cowpens, Morgan and his troops marched northward to North Carolina. There, they rejoined another part of the Continental army, led by General Nathanael Greene. Greene hoped that the British, commanded by General Cornwallis, would follow him. He wanted to pull Cornwallis farther and farther away from his base of supplies at Charles Town.

Cornwallis took the bait and chased Greene's army across North Carolina. The British and Americans fought bloody battles across the state. Finally, Cornwallis headed to Yorktown, on the coast of Virginia. He hoped to get supplies from a British fleet there. Instead, he was trapped at Yorktown by General Washington's army and French troops that had become allies of the Americans. The British army was forced to surrender on October 19, 1781. This was the last major battle of the Revolutionary War. The Americans had won their independence, and now Delaware and the twelve other states faced the difficult job of creating a new nation.

The First State

Following the Revolutionary War, the thirteen states were governed by a set of rules known as the Articles of Confederation. The articles had been approved during the war. But the federal, or central, government that they established was weak, with only limited power. There was no president and the national congress could do little.

By the mid-1780s, many political leaders recognized that the new country needed a stronger form of centralized government. A convention was called at Philadelphia in 1787 to improve the Articles of Confederation. Instead of making improvements, the convention ended up writing a new document, the U.S. Constitution.

Benjamin Franklin and Alexander Hamilton were among the delegates to the Constitutional Convention who debated issues with the delegates from Delaware.

Delaware sent five delegates to that convention: George Read; Richard Bassett, a lawyer and landowner; Jacob Broom, a merchant from Wilmington; Gunning Bedford Jr., the state's attorney general; and John Dickinson. These men recognized that the national government needed changing. But they also wanted to be sure that small states, like Delaware, were not overpowered by large ones that might have more representatives in Congress.

At the convention, Dickinson helped develop a plan called the Great Compromise. This plan called for two houses of Congress. The states would have equal representation in one, the Senate. In the other, the House of Representatives, the large states would have more representatives than the small states.

When the new Constitution was complete, a copy was sent to each of the states for ratification (approval). On December 3, 1787, a Delaware convention met at Dover to consider the new document. Four days later, the delegates approved the Constitution unanimously. Delaware became the first state to ratify the new government. Today, Delaware is still known as "the First State."

Delaware's journey from colony to state is a story of bravery, tolerance, and growth. The story lasted from Delaware's humble beginnings as a part of Pennsylvania to the fight of its brave soldiers during the Revolutionary War. Though small, the First State has always had a generous heart and great courage.

Recipe
Snickerdoodles

Colonists loved sweet treats as much as we do today. One treat with a funny name came from Dutch settlers in New Netherland and spread throughout the colonies. It was a small cookie called a snickerdoodle.

1/2 cup butter or margarine
3/4 cup sugar
1 egg
2 cups flour
1 1/2 teaspoons baking powder
1/2 teaspoon salt
1/2 cup milk
1/2 teaspoon vanilla extract
2 tablespoons sugar
2 teaspoons cinnamon

- Preheat oven to 325 degrees.
- Press the butter in a mixing bowl with a wooden spoon until smooth.
- Add the sugar to the butter, and mix thoroughly.
- Add the egg. Beat butter, sugar, and egg mixture well.
- Mix the flour, baking powder, and salt in a bowl.
- Combine the milk and vanilla.
- Add 1/3 of the flour mixture to the butter mixture. Blend until smooth.
- Add 1/2 of the milk mixture. Blend until smooth.
- Add another 1/3 of the flour mixture.
- Add the remaining 1/2 of the milk mixture. Mix well.
- Add the last 1/3 of the flour mixture. Mix until the dough is smooth.
- Combine 2 tablespoons sugar and 2 teaspoons cinnamon in a small bowl.
- Butter a large cookie tray. Place teaspoonfuls of dough on it about 2 inches apart.
- Sprinkle the dough with the cinnamon and sugar mixture.
- Bake cookies for about 15 minutes or until the edges are golden brown.
- Remove cookies and place them on a cooling rack.

This activity should be done with adult supervision.

Activity
Quill Pen and Ink

Colonists could not run down to the corner store to buy a new pen or pencil with which to write. They had to make their own writing utensils. Here is a simple way to make ink and a quill pen like those used by the colonists.

Procedure

Large turkey, peacock, or pheasant feather (may be bought at a craft store) • Scissors or penknife 10 walnut shells • 1 cup water 1/2 teaspoon vinegar • 1/2 teaspoon salt Hammer • Old cloth/rag • Saucepan Small jar with lid • Strainer

- Wrap the shells in the cloth and crush them with the hammer.
- Put the crushed shells and water in the saucepan and boil the mixture for about 45 minutes. (Most of the water will evaporate.)
- Let the ink mixture cool.
- Pour the mixture through the strainer into the jar.
- Add vinegar and salt.
- Cut the quill end of the feather at a 45 degree angle with the scissors or a penknife.
- Dip the pen in the ink and write.

This activity should be done with adult supervision.

Delaware

Time Line

1524 Giovanni da Verrazano sails past Delaware Bay.

1610 Samuel Argall names Delaware Bay after Virginia governor De La Warr.

1631 Dutch settlers arrive aboard the Whale.

1643 Johan Printz becomes governor of New Sweden.

1664 English take over Delaware.

1500   1525   1625   1650   1675

1609 Henry Hudson sails into Delaware Bay and claims territory for the Dutch.

1626 Dutch settlers arrive from New Netherland.

1632 Swedish settlement of Fort Christina is established.

1655 Dutch take over New Sweden.

1681 William Penn claims Delaware colony.

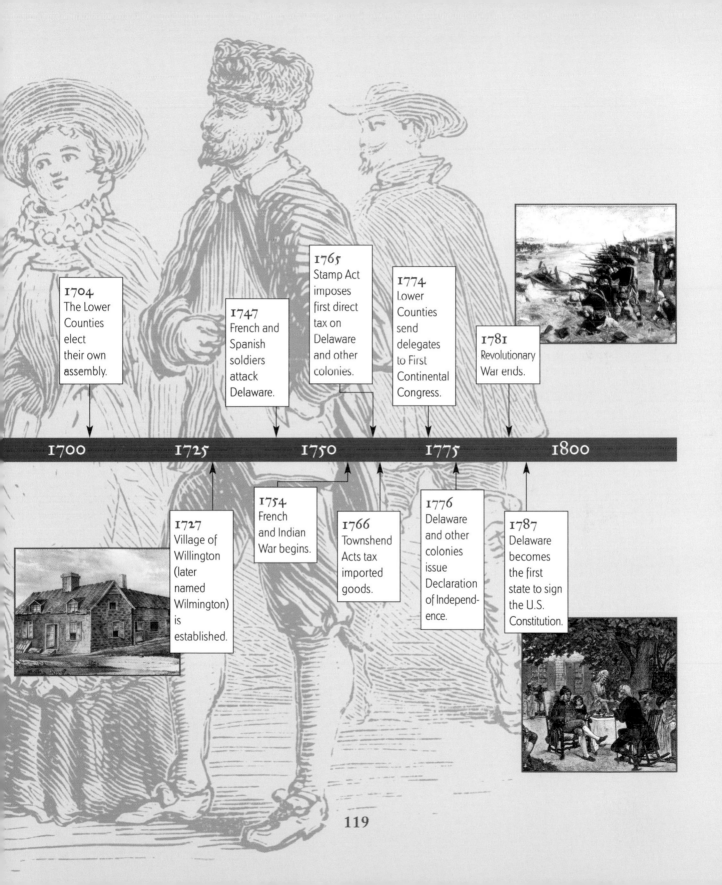

1704
The Lower Counties elect their own assembly.

1747
French and Spanish soldiers attack Delaware.

1765
Stamp Act imposes first direct tax on Delaware and other colonies.

1774
Lower Counties send delegates to First Continental Congress.

1781
Revolutionary War ends.

1700   **1725**   **1750**   **1775**   **1800**

1727
Village of Willington (later named Wilmington) is established.

1754
French and Indian War begins.

1766
Townshend Acts tax imported goods.

1776
Delaware and other colonies issue Declaration of Independence.

1787
Delaware becomes the first state to sign the U.S. Constitution.

119

Further Reading

Flower, Milton. *John Dickinson: Conservative Revolutionary.* Charlottesville: University Press of Virginia, 1983.

Hoffecker, Carol. *Delaware, The First State.* Middle Atlantic Press, 1988.

Melchiore, Susan McCarthy. *Caesar Rodney: American Patriot.* Philadelphia: Chelsea House, 2001.

Munroe, John. *Colonial Delaware: A History.* Millwood, NY: KTO Press, 1978.

Glossary

abolish to put an end to, stop

abstain to stop yourself from doing something

allegiance loyalty to one's country

ally to enter into a pact with someone or a country

artillery powerful guns attached to wheels or tracks

artisan one who is skilled at a craft

boycott agreement not to buy from and sell to a person or country

buckskin soft leather created from the skin of a deer

constitution a set of laws that are used as a country's legal standard

debt money owed to another

delegate a representative to a conference or convention

democratic favoring the rule of a country by the people

empire large group of states controlled by one ruler

expedition voyage or journey undertaken to accomplish a goal

frontier the outer limits of settled land

immigrant a person who comes to live in a foreign
  country

independent self-governing, not allied with another
  government

intolerant not accepting of the differences of others

migrate to move from one locality to another

militia an army made up of ordinary citizens instead of
  professional soldiers

outpost a frontier military base or settlement

parlor a room designed to receive guests

pelt the skin of a fur-bearing animal

plowshare the blade of a plow used to dig into the ground

privateer owner of a privately owned ship hired by a
  government to attack its enemies

refuge a safe haven, protection from danger

spirituality having to do with the soul

unanimous having the agreement of all involved

volley firing by many weapons at once

Index